Countries Around the World
Wales

Mary Colson

www.raintreepublishers.co.uk
Visit our website to find out
more information about
Raintree books.

To order:
☎ Phone 0845 6044371
🖨 Fax +44 (0) 1865 312263
📧 Email myorders@raintreepublishers.co.uk

Customers from outside the UK please telephone +44 1865 312262

Raintree is an imprint of **Capstone Global Library Limited**, a
company incorporated in England and Wales having its registered
office at 7 Pilgrim Street, London, EC4V 6LB – Registered company
number: 6695582

Edited by Louise Galpine, Kate DeVilliers, and Laura Knowles
Designed by Richard Parker
Original illustrations © Capstone Global Library Ltd 2011
Illustrated by Oxford Designers & Illustrators
Picture research by Liz Alexander
Originated by Capstone Global Library Ltd
Printed in China by CTPS

ISBN 978 1 406 22804 5 (hardback)
15 14 13 12 11
10 9 8 7 6 5 4 3 2 1

ISBN 978 1 406 22833 5 (paperback)
16 15 14 13 12
10 9 8 7 6 5 4 3 2 1

British Library Cataloguing in Publication Data
Colson, Mary.
Wales. -- (Countries around the world)
942.9'086-dc22
A full catalogue record for this book is available from the British
Library.

Acknowledgments
We would like to thank the following for permission to reproduce
photographs: Alamy pp. 25 (© Jeff Morgan 07), 33 (© ffotowales);
Corbis pp. 10 (© Hulton-Deutsch Collection), 22 (© Construction
Photography), 29 (© Pool/Christian Liewig/Liewig Media Sports),
32 (© Andrew Fox), 36 (© Frank Trapper); Getty Images pp. 9
(Hulton Archive), 26 (Brian Seed/Time Life Pictures); iStockphoto
p. 11 (© Matthew Dixon); Mary Evans Picture Library p. 7 (Edwin
Mullan Collection); Photolibrary pp. 17 (John Warburton-Lee
Photography), 35 (Joff Lee/Fresh Food Images); Shutterstock pp. 5
(© Len Green), 6 (© Marina Kryukova), 13 (© Alan Bryant), 15
(© Lee O'Dell), 19 (© Gail Johnson), 21 (© eldo), 27 (© Alistair
Scott), 30 (© Tim Dobbs), 37 (© Gail Johnson), 39 (© Len Green),
46 (© granata1111).

Cover photograph of a man jumping off a rock reproduced with
permission of Photolibrary/Philip Lee Harvey/Cultura.

We would like to thank Rob Bowden and Ann and John Thomas for
their invaluable help in the preparation of this book.

Every effort has been made to contact copyright holders of material
reproduced in this book. Any omissions will be rectified in
subsequent printings if notice is given to the publisher.

Contents

Some words are printed in bold, **like this**. You can find out what they mean by looking in the glossary.

Introducing Wales

What do you think of when you think of Wales? Do you see dragons and daffodils? Or do you think of ruined castles and rushing rivers?

Wales is one of the four countries that make up the United Kingdom (UK) of **Great Britain** and Northern Ireland. With a landscape carved by glaciers, it is a country of jagged mountains, deep valleys, natural lakes, and fertile pastures. Wales has a unique **culture**, its own language, and a very **turbulent** history.

Language matters

Out of a population of nearly three million, over half a million people speak Welsh as their first language and English second. S4C is the Welsh language TV channel. Its most popular programme is the soap opera *Pobol y Cwm* (People of the Valley).

How to say...

welcome to Wales	*croeso i Gymru*	(croesoh ee gum-ree)
good morning	*bore da*	(bore-ay dar)
my name is…	*fy enw i yw…*	(vu aynoo e ew)
how are you?	*sut mae?*	(shum my)
fine, thank you	*lawn diolch*	(yeown dee-olch)
goodbye	*da bo ti*	(dar bow tee)

Cultural life

Wales has produced many poets, musicians, and writers. The Welsh are also passionate about **rugby**. The players in the national team are treated like superstars.

The patron saint of Wales is St David. On St David's Day, 1 March, Welsh people all over the world wear a leek or a daffodil. The national flag is *Y Ddraig Goch* (uhh thry goch), which means "The Red Dragon".

Mount Snowdon is the highest mountain in Wales at 1,085 metres (3,559 feet). Its name means "snow hill".

History: becoming Wales

Today Wales is a peaceful country, but Welsh history is full of bloody battles and stories of courage and resistance.

Before the Romans occupied much of modern-day England and Wales from AD 43, Wales was inhabited by Celts. The Celts were farmers and craftsmen who made beautiful jewellery out of the gold they found in the mountains. After taking the gold, the Romans left, never fully conquering the Celts.

A land of kings

After the Romans, the Anglo-Saxons invaded from England and the Vikings attacked from the sea. A number of kingdoms formed in the area now called Wales, each with a different leader. The first man to rule a considerable part of Wales was Rhodri Mawr (Rhodri the Great). Over many centuries, the Welsh kings defended their lands against English and Viking forces.

Caerphilly Castle is the largest castle in Wales.

Llywelyn the Last gave himself the title of Prince of Wales in 1258. This painting shows the moment he was killed by an English soldier.

English power

The Welsh kingdoms fought each other for power and land. At the same time, English forces were trying to gain Welsh lands. Gradually, more and more kingdoms came under English control. In 1282, the death of Llywelyn the Last led to the **conquest** of Wales by King Edward I of England.

THE PRINCE OF WALES

The first official Prince of Wales was Llywelyn the Last (1248–1282). He fought against the English and tried to reclaim Welsh lands. Today, the title "Prince of Wales" is given to the heir to the British throne. Prince Charles is the current Prince of Wales and when he becomes King, Prince William will hold the title.

Ruled by the enemy

Welsh **medieval** history is dominated by English aggression and Welsh resistance. English **nobles** built castles in Wales to establish **colonies** and extend their control.

Political language

The Statute of Rhuddlan in 1284 officially united England and Wales under English rule. Later acts in 1536 and 1542 increased English control and English became the official language of business in Wales. Welsh was banned from being spoken in government jobs and people were forced to learn English if they wanted to **hold office**. Welsh did not become an official language of Wales again until 1942.

Welsh hero

Unhappy with the union, the Welsh launched several revolts against English rule, including one on 16 September 1400 led by Owain Glyndŵr. Although initially successful, the uprising was eventually put down. Glyndŵr was never captured and was last seen in 1412.

TWM SIÔN CATI (AROUND 1530–1620)

Known as the Welsh Robin Hood, Twm Siôn Cati robbed the rich to give to the poor. Twm's exploits as a robber and horse thief became legendary throughout Wales. It is said that at night his ghost still rides near the cave he used as a hideout.

Heroines of Abergwaun

In 1797 the townswomen of Abergwaun spotted a French fleet off the Welsh coast. The local soldiers were away so the women dressed in traditional Welsh dress with tall black hats, black skirts, and red shawls and armed themselves with farm tools. The French saw the soldiers on the cliffs and held back. The real soldiers returned and the French surrendered to the two armies.

Owain Glyndŵr was the last native Welshman to be Prince of Wales.

English government

In 1707, Scotland was also joined with England and Wales. Together, the three countries became the United Kingdom of **Great Britain**, with government based in London. Since then Wales has become an **industrialized**, **multicultural** country and has seen its political status change too.

Powering the nation

From the late 1700s to the 1920s, Wales experienced rapid industrialization and a dramatic rise in population as a result of the fast-growing coal, iron, and steel industries. The UK was in the middle of its **Industrial Revolution** and coal was needed to power factories and transport across the nation. Coal miners and their families faced a grim existence, with thousands dying in mining accidents.

The economic depression of the 1930s hit Wales hard and traditional industries declined. Half a million people left Wales between 1920 and 1940 to find work. By the 1980s, very few mines were still working and **unemployment** was high.

It wasn't only men who worked in the coal industry. Women and children worked 12-hour shifts in the mines.

The road to self-rule

In 1964 the first Secretary of State for Wales was appointed and in 1999 the Welsh Assembly was established. This gave Wales a government of its own. After hundreds of years of English rule, today Wales makes many of its own decisions.

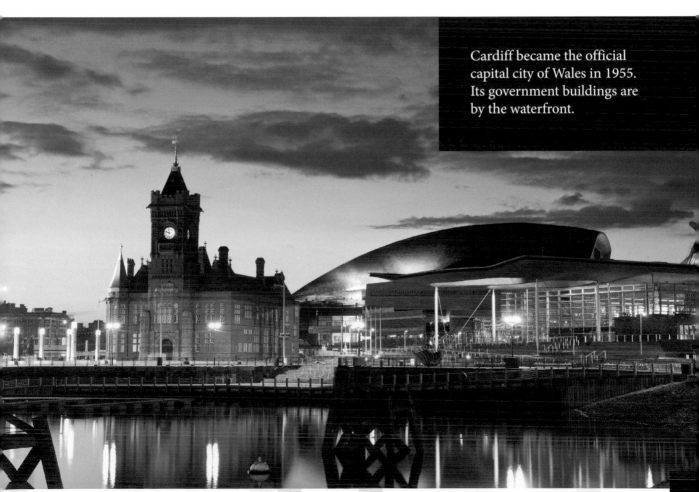

Cardiff became the official capital city of Wales in 1955. Its government buildings are by the waterfront.

Regions and resources: water world and working life

Wales is a small country of 21,588 square kilometres (8,335 square miles). There are over 60 offshore islands, the largest of which is Anglesey, across the Menai Straits.

The landscape of Wales is dominated by mountains that stretch the length of the country from the Brecon Beacons in the south to the peaks of Snowdonia in the north. Rivers such as the Severn, the Wye, and the Usk criss-cross the scenery.

Coastal wonder

Perhaps the most striking feature in Wales is its jagged coastline, which is 1,208 kilometres (750 miles) long and dotted with beaches. The Irish Sea lies on the northern border, with St George's Channel to the west, and the Bristol Channel to the south. The seas around the country support a huge variety of **marine** life and some small-scale fishing. Wales only has 257 kilometres (160 miles) of land border, which it shares with England.

This map shows the key towns and landscape features of Wales.

The beautiful Gower coastline is a major attraction of south Wales.

Offa's Dyke

Offa was an English king in the ad 700s who decided to build an earth barrier along the border of England and Wales as a means of defence against the Welsh. The barrier, known as a dyke, was about 27 metres (88 feet) wide and 8 metres (26 feet) high. Much of it is still visible today.

Weather report

Famous for being cloudy, wet and windy, Wales has a temperate climate, which means that it never gets very hot or very cold. June, July, and August are the warmest months, whilst January is the coldest.

Wild landscape

Much of Wales is very mountainous and only a small amount of the population lives in the countryside. The **rural** areas are generally poorer than towns and cities, where there is more chance of employment. In the southern towns of Swansea, Newport, and Cardiff, there are many **insurance** companies, electronics factories, and government offices. Mining for coal and even gold continues on a small scale.

Waterland

The middle of the country is full of hills, lakes, and waterfalls. The highest waterfall is Pistyll Rhaeadr, which is higher than Niagara Falls. Mid-Wales has no large cities but there are small spa towns like Llandrindod Wells. There are also many reservoirs here that feed the area's **hydroelectric** power stations.

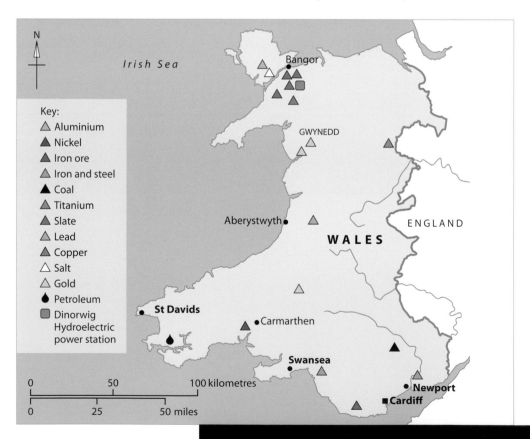

Use the key on this map to find out where different natural resources come from in Wales.

Sheepdogs herd sheep that graze on moorland and mountain pastures.

Livestock farming

Due to poor-quality soil and hilly landscape, much of Wales is unsuitable for crop-growing, so livestock farming is more common. Sheep farming happens mostly in the mountains and moorlands, with dairy farming around the coast.

Daily life

There are more than 11 million sheep in Wales. Farmers use Welsh sheepdogs to round up their flocks for shearing and to go to market. The highly skilled dogs herd the sheep by following voice or whistle signals from the farmer.

Economic status

The Welsh **economy** is interlinked with the British economy, with **policies** decided in London and Cardiff. The British government has attracted **multinational** companies to Wales with generous **incentives** but **unemployment** is still higher than the UK average and salaries are lower.

YOUNG PEOPLE

Youth unemployment is a big issue in Wales with 45 per cent of unemployed people aged under 25. Some young people find work in call centres, factories, or in government offices but many leave Wales and go to live and work in England.

Minting money

Wales uses the pound sterling as its **currency**, like the rest of the United Kingdom. The symbol is £ and the central bank is the Bank of England. The Royal Mint, which produces all the coins in the UK, is based at Llantrisant in south Wales.

How to say...

sheep	*dafad*	(davvad)	**field**	*cae*	(kye)
cow	*buwch*	(bewch)	**farmer**	*ffarmwr*	(farmoor)
dog	*ci*	(key)	**river**	*afon*	(arvon)
hill	*bryn*	(brin)	**mountain**	*mynydd*	(menaith)

Castles

Home to Snowdonia National Park, North Wales boasts four castles with **World Heritage** status. Caernarfon and Harlech are the most famous of these. This combination of natural wonders and exciting history gives North Wales its important tourism industry.

Old and new

The Welsh economy has adapted to change. The castles are now visitor centres and the old mining railroads now carry visitors on day trips. Welsh industry today includes specialist car and aircraft factories, as well as electronics manufacturing. Airbus and Sony have factories in Wales.

Dinorwig power station was built inside a mountain. Much of the electricity **generated** by Wales' large hydroelectric power stations is sold to English electricity companies.

Wildlife: protecting nature

Because weather in Wales is often harsh, with gales blowing in from the Irish Sea, Welsh animals are **bred** to be hardy. Native animals, such as Welsh black cattle, live happily on rugged hillsides. Dolwen sheep graze in windy pastures and Welsh mountain ponies survive high up in rocky **terrain**.

Royal favourite

Perhaps one of the most famous animals associated with Wales is the corgi. Corgis were bred to herd cattle up to Smithfield Market in London along the old **drovers'** roads. The corgi is a short-legged dog that nipped the heels of the cattle to keep them moving along. Queen Elizabeth II has kept many corgis as pets.

Under threat

With environmental pollution, wind farm construction, and wetlands being destroyed, many native birds are under threat. The Common Scoter duck, the Black Grouse, and the song thrush are all listed as **endangered**. Steps are now being taken to help their survival by preserving their **habitats**. New building developments near their nesting grounds are now banned.

How to say...

animal	anifail	(anivial)
pony	merlyn	(mairlin)
rabbit	cwningen	(cooningen)
eagle	eryr	(airoor)
bird	aderyn	(aderin)
duck	hwyaded	(who-ee-yadin)
deer	carw	(karoo)
dolphin	dolffin	(dolfin)

YOUNG PEOPLE

Many Welsh children are involved in conservation groups, such as the Wildlife Trust and the Sea Trust. **Marine** life is at risk from cargo ships and fishing nets along the Welsh coast. Children help to carry out dolphin and seabird surveys, as well as learn about how to protect the marine environment.

In Snowdonia National Park, small herds of Welsh mountain ponies roam free.

Managing the environment

The Environment Agency of England and Wales oversees the use of land and **resources** in the country. It tries to make sure that all development is **sustainable** and affects the environment as little as possible. Waste Awareness Wales (WAW) is the department of the Welsh Assembly that tells the public about local recycling schemes and manages household waste. Each house in Wales has different coloured plastic bins for their recycling.

National Parks

There are three national parks in Wales, covering an area of 4,122 square kilometres (1,592 square miles), about a fifth of the country. Snowdonia, the Pembrokeshire Coast, and the Brecon Beacons National Parks contain some of the most beautiful landscapes in the whole of the UK. They are protected areas. In the UK people live, work, and go to school in national parks and you don't have to pay to enter them.

Eco-research

In 1973 the Centre for Alternative Technology (CAT) was founded in a **disused** slate mine. CAT researches environmental issues that affect the world, such as climate change, pollution, and using resources. Staff and volunteers live at the centre using **renewable** energy sources, such as wind power. They grow their own food by farming in a sustainable way.

YOUNG PEOPLE

WAW runs an Eco-Schools programme across Wales to raise environmental awareness. Pupils set up eco-committees with parents and staff and then create an action plan that outlines how they are going to help the environment. Some schools have banned plastic bags whilst others have planted trees or created wildlife areas.

Between 2010 and 2020, 23 more wind farms will be built in Wales.

Infrastructure: politics and people

In 1404, Owain Glyndŵr held the first Welsh **parliament** in the town of Machynlleth. Nearly 600 years later, Wales has its own government once again. In 1997, Welsh people **voted** for **devolution** from the rest of the United Kingdom, and in 1999 the National Assembly for Wales met for the first time.

The Senedd

The Senedd or Senate is where the Assembly meets every week to discuss issues that are important to Wales and Welsh people. You can watch the debates in person from the Senedd's public gallery or on the Senedd website.

The Assembly is made up of 60 **elected** Assembly Members who represent different **constituencies**. The Members belong to different political parties and are voted in every four years. Anyone over the age of 18 can vote. The Assembly is led by the Presiding Officer who is elected by its members. There are four main parties in the Welsh Assembly: Welsh Labour, the Welsh Liberal Democrats, the Welsh Conservative Party, and Plaid Cymru, the Welsh **Nationalist** Party.

The Senedd building is in Cardiff.

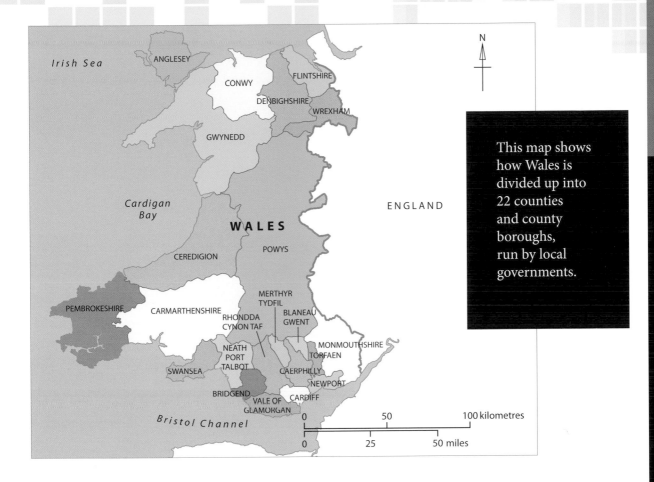

Irish Sea

ANGLESEY

CONWY

FLINTSHIRE

DENBIGHSHIRE

WREXHAM

GWYNEDD

Cardigan Bay

WALES

ENGLAND

CEREDIGION

POWYS

MERTHYR TYDFIL

PEMBROKESHIRE

CARMARTHENSHIRE

RHONDDA CYNON TAF

BLANEAU GWENT

MONMOUTHSHIRE

NEATH PORT TALBOT

TORFAEN

SWANSEA

CAERPHILLY

NEWPORT

BRIDGEND

CARDIFF

VALE OF GLAMORGAN

Bristol Channel

0   50   100 kilometres

0   25   50 miles

N

This map shows how Wales is divided up into 22 counties and county boroughs, run by local governments.

Two-tier government

The National Assembly for Wales nominates a First Minister to form and lead the Welsh Assembly Government. The government works with the National Assembly to create measures (laws) in some areas, such as health, education and agriculture. Wales does not control all of its laws however and is still affected by laws made by the UK parliament in London. There are 40 Welsh Members of Parliament in the UK parliament.

YOUNG PEOPLE

Plaid Cymru has a youth group called CymruX. Members go to meetings and conferences to discuss issues they care about with other young people and party leaders. CymruX encourages young people to get involved in the political process.

School life

Welsh children start elementary school at five years old. Between the ages of 11 and 16 they go to high school. Pupils learn a wide range of subjects including English, maths, science, history, geography, art, music, and drama. About a fifth of schools in Wales teach children all their subjects in Welsh.

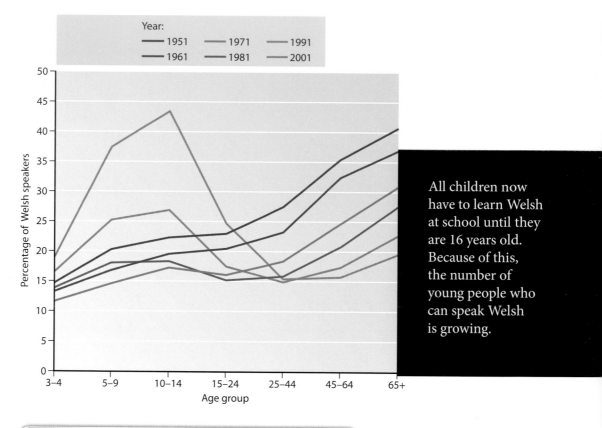

All children now have to learn Welsh at school until they are 16 years old. Because of this, the number of young people who can speak Welsh is growing.

How to say...

Welsh	*Cymraeg*	(cumryg)
English	*Saesneg*	(sisneg)
maths	*mathemateg*	(mattamateg)
art	*ystryw*	(us-strew)
sport	*sbort*	(sbort)
music	*cerdd*	(kairth)

Daily life

Most elementary schools begin the day at 9 a.m. with the whole school gathering for an assembly. In the assembly there could be notices, singing, and prayers. Children usually eat lunch at school. They take a packed lunch from home or pay for a hot meal. Some children eat their breakfast at school. The school day ends between 3.00 p.m. and 3.30 p.m. Many schools run homework clubs or after-school activity clubs.

At the age of 16, pupils take **national exams**. The results decide whether they stay on at school to study for A-levels and university entry, get a job, or study on a **vocational course**.

School uniform is common in Welsh schools.

Housing and health

Most people in Wales live in modern brick houses on housing developments, in glass and steel blocks of flats, or in old **terraced houses**. In the countryside, beautiful cottages are common.

One-night houses

In the 1700s, a rise in population and a lack of houses forced many people to squat on common land. The *tŷ unnos* custom said that you could own the land provided your house was built overnight and smoke was rising from the chimney in the morning. The original **turf** and **thatch** dwellings were later rebuilt in stone and the cottages are still lived in today.

ANEURIN BEVAN (1897–1960)

Aneurin Bevan is known as the "Father of the NHS". Born into a poor mining family in south Wales, Bevan saw the impact of poverty and disease on people's lives. He won a **scholarship** to study in London where he went into politics. He established the NHS in 1948.

Health matters

In the UK, every person is registered to a doctor. If you are ill, you make an appointment and see the doctor free of charge. In Wales, **prescriptions**, hospital treatment ,and operations are free. The National Health Service (NHS) works by providing medical services when people need them and not depending on whether they can pay. The NHS employs over 90,000 people across Wales.

Some people in Wales live in traditional country cottages.

Culture: national identities

Welsh people are passionate about sport. Climbing in Snowdonia, hiking along the Gower coastal path, and mountain biking in Afan Forest are popular activities. Wales has hosted many important sports events including the Rugby World Cup and golf's Ryder Cup.

Sports stars

Wales has many famous sportspeople, including footballer Ryan Giggs, cyclists Nicole Cooke and Geraint Thomas, and golfer Ian Woosnam. Rugby is the national sport and players such as Stephen Jones and Shane Williams are treated like celebrities wherever they go.

National pride

The Welsh national anthem was written in 1856 by Evan James and his son. In 1905 it became the first national anthem to be sung before a sporting event when Wales were playing the New Zealand All Blacks at rugby. This is the first verse:

Mae hen wlad fy nhadau yn annwyl i mi,
Gwlad beirdd a chantorion, enwogion o fri;
Ei gwrol ryfelwyr, gwladgarwyr tra mâd,
Tros ryddid gollasant eu gwaed.

The land of my fathers, the land of my choice,
*The land in which poets and **minstrels** rejoice;*
The land whose stern warriors were true to the core,
*While bleeding for freedom **of yore**.*

The Millennium Stadium in Cardiff is the home ground of the Welsh national rugby team. Here they are celebrating after winning against France in 2008.

National holidays

In Wales and the rest of the United Kingdom, national holidays are known as bank holidays. By law, banks are required to close on these days. There are eight each year, including Christmas Day and Easter Monday. Most people have a holiday from work on these days.

Capital of culture

Wales' largest city is also its capital. Multicultural Cardiff is home to more than 320,000 people. Because of the busy port the city has well-established Italian, Maltese, and Somali communities today.

Cardiff is a vibrant, modern city. One of the newest buildings is the Wales Millennium Centre which hosts concerts and exhibitions, and is home to the Welsh National Opera. Cardiff's castle dominates the city centre and the many museums preserve the nation's history.

One of the most popular places in the city is the Techniquest Science Discovery Centre. Children and adults can learn about science, computers, and technology through the interactive activities here.

The Wales Millennium Centre in Cardiff has special windows that spell out two short poems, one in Welsh and one in English.

Religious groups

Christianity is the largest religion in Wales, with many Catholic and Baptist churches. There are six cathedrals in Wales, some dating back to the 6th century. Today, less than 10 per cent of the population attends church regularly. There are many other faiths practised in Wales, including Islam. The first mosque in the UK opened in Cardiff in 1860 and now there are more than 40 around the country.

This chart shows the main faith groups in Wales today.

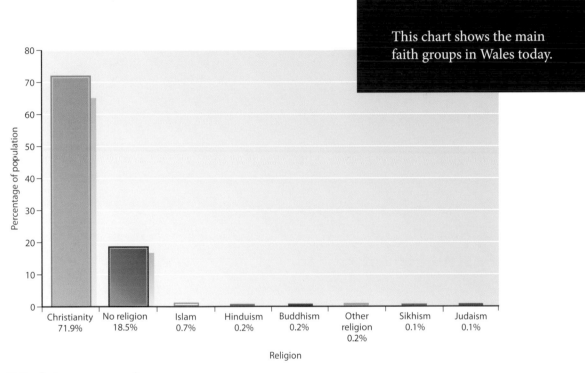

Religion

Making music

With a culture of hymn-writing and choirs, music is an important part of Welsh life. Traditional welsh music is kept alive through many male voice choirs. Folk music is also popular and can be heard at one of the many *gŵyl werin* (festivals). Opera singer Bryn Terfel and stars like Tom Jones, the Manic Street Preachers, and Stereophonics have all made their mark on the global stage.

Celebrating the arts

Wales is a story-telling nation, rich in myths and legends. The medieval *Mabinogion* is a collection of Welsh folk tales. "The Bells of Aberdovey" is a popular story about a village **submerged** in Cardigan Bay. The story says that the church bells can still be heard ringing beneath the waves.

One of the earliest Welsh writers was the poet Taliesin in the 6th century. He wrote poems about King Arthur. Modern Welsh writers include Roald Dahl, author of *Fantastic Mr Fox*. He was born in Cardiff to Norwegian parents.

DYLAN THOMAS (1914–1953)

Dylan Thomas is one of the most famous Welsh writers. His story, *A Child's Christmas in Wales*, describes life in rural Wales. His most famous work is the radio play *Under Milk Wood*, which is set in a Welsh seaside town.

Festival town

Every year, the small Welsh town of Hay-on-Wye becomes the centre of the literary world as it hosts a large book festival. Over 80,000 people come to the town to visit the 30 bookshops and hear writers talk about their work.

The Hay Festival has grown very popular since it began in 1988.

National show

For over a thousand years, Welsh people have celebrated the arts at special festivals called *eisteddfods*. When Wales was ruled by England, eisteddfods were a way of keeping Welsh culture alive. Choir singing, acting, dancing, and poetry are just some of the activities on show.

Traditional ceremonies are performed during the National Eisteddfod of Wales. Here, a young woman is carrying a Horn of Plenty.

YOUNG PEOPLE

The Urdd is a national arts and activity organization with over 50,000 members in Wales. Members take part in various activities including writing, musical performances, and outdoor pursuits.

A festival of food

Many Welsh towns hold food festivals to celebrate local produce. The national food festival takes place in Welshpool in September.

One of the more unusual Welsh foods is *bara lawr* or laverbread. It isn't bread at all, but boiled seaweed! Laverbread is traditionally fried and eaten with bacon and **cockles** for breakfast. Laverbread is very nutritious as it's rich in iron.

There are lots of popular Welsh cakes including *bara brith*, which is a fruit bread. The traditional meat for dinner is Welsh lamb, which sometimes has a sweet, salty taste due to lambs grazing on **estuary** land. Welsh rarebit is a good snack. This is toast topped with a mixture of cheese, mustard, and beer.

How to say...

bread	*bara*	(barra)
butter	*menyn*	(mayneen)
cheese	*caws*	(cows)
fruit	*ffrwyth*	(freuyth)
apple	*afa*	(aval)
salt	*halen*	(hallen)
cake	*cacen*	(ka-ken)
biscuit	*bisged*	(bisk-ed)
sugar	*siwgr*	(shoo-gur)
beer	*cwrw*	(cour-roo)
water	*dŵr*	(doo-er)

Welsh cakes

Ask an adult to help you make this delicious treat.

Ingredients

- 225 grams self-raising flour, sieved
- 10 grams salted butter
- 85 grams caster sugar
- handful of sultanas
- 1 egg
- milk (if needed)
- extra butter for greasing

What to do

1. Rub the butter into the sieved flour to make crumbs.
2. Add the sugar, dried fruit, and then the egg. Mix to combine, then form a ball of dough using a splash of milk if needed.
3. Roll out the pastry until it is 5millimetres (¼ inch) thick. Cut into rounds with a 7.5–10 centimetres (3–4 inch) cutter.
4. Heat a frying pan and melt a little butter. Place the cakes on the pan, turning once. Cook for 2 to 3 minutes on each side until they are light brown.
5. Remove from the pan and dust with caster sugar while still warm.

Wales today

After centuries of struggle, today Wales is stepping out from the shadow of its English neighbour. With increasing control over its own decisions, and pride in its language and culture, Wales is raising its global profile. Welsh communities around the world are keeping Welsh traditions and customs alive, too. St David's Day celebrations can be seen across the United States and Canada. There are also Welsh-speaking communities in Argentina.

Welsh actress Catherine Zeta Jones won an Oscar in 2008.

Lights, camera, action!

The Welsh film industry is thriving. Cardiff has the second largest media centre and film studio in the UK. Popular science fiction programmes, such as *Torchwood* and *Doctor Who*, are filmed here. Welsh actors are now successful in Hollywood with some, such as Anthony Hopkins and Catherine Zeta-Jones, winning Oscars.

Cultural appeal

Millions of tourists visit Wales each year to experience the hospitality of its people and to visit its landmarks and natural wonders. The English-built castles that were once used to control the Welsh now give Wales a priceless national tourist attraction. Wales has more castles per square kilometre than any other country in Western Europe.

Caernarfon Castle (see map on page 12) is one of the most famous in Wales. It attracts many tourists every year, and has been named a World Heritage Site.

Emerging nation

Wales doesn't yet have a full parliament with the power to create its own laws independently, but it does have a governing assembly. Unemployment is high, the economic problems are large, and **social inequality** is a serious issue in some parts of the country. Modern Wales faces many of the same challenges as other developed nations. For the first time in its history, the country has got the power to start solving some of them itself.

Fact file

Official languages:	Welsh, English
Capital city:	Cardiff
Bordering country:	England
Population:	2,993,000
Largest cities in terms of population:	Cardiff, Newport, Swansea
Life expectancy:	76.6 years for men; 81.8 years for women
Religions:	Christianity, Islam, Hinduism, Judaism
National symbols:	dragon, leek, daffodil
Total area:	21,588 square kilometres (8,335 square miles)
Major rivers:	Severn, Wye, Dee, Usk
Highest point:	Mount Snowdon at 1,085 metres (3,559 feet)
Climate:	temperate

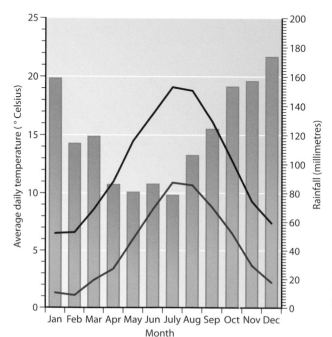

This chart shows the average rainfall and highest and lowest temperatures each month in Wales.

Key:

— Temperature (maximum)
— Temperature (minimum)
■ Rainfall

Currency:	pound sterling
Natural resources:	coal, slate, lead, copper
Imports and exports:	electricity, food, manufactured goods, oil, gas, dairy products
Major industries:	tourism, public services, electronics, technology
Literacy rates:	99 per cent of the population can read and write
Units of measurement:	metric
World Heritage sites:	Blaenavon Industrial Landscape, Pontcysyllte Aquaduct, Beaumaris Castle, Caernarfon Castle, Conwy Castle, Harlech Castle
Large Welsh populations elsewhere:	Argentine Patagonia
Festivals:	Hay-on-Wye literature festival, National Eisteddfod, Welsh Food Festival, St David's Day
Famous people:	Ryan Giggs (footballer), Shane Williams (rugby player), Nicole Cooke (cyclist), Tanni Grey-Thompson (Paralympic athlete), Geraint Thomas (cyclist), Tom Jones (singer), Katherine Jenkins (singer), Catherine Zeta Jones (actor), Rhys Ifans (actor), Anthony Hopkins (actor), Dylan Thomas (poet), Roald Dahl (writer), Rob Brydon (comedian), Rowan Williams (Archbishop of Canterbury), Laura Ashley (businesswoman)

Have a go at saying the longest place name in Wales! The name means "Saint Mary's Church in the Hollow of the White Hazel Near a Rapid Whirlpool and the Church of Saint Tysilio of the Red Cave".

Timeline

AD is short for *Anno Domini*, which is Latin for "in the year of our Lord". AD is added before a date and means that the date occurred after the birth of Jesus Christ, for example, AD 720.

AD 43	The Romans invade Britain. Some of the people living in Wales, the Celts, are driven west to Ireland.
around AD 870	Rhodri Mawr (Rhodri The Great) is the first man to rule a large part of Wales
around 1200–1240	Llywelyn the Last gives himself the title Prince of Wales. He fights against the English and tries to reclaim Welsh lands.
1268–1271	Caerphilly Castle is built by an English nobleman to stop the Welsh moving into English lands. This leads to a dispute between Llywelyn the Last and Edward I of England.
1282	Death of Llywelyn the Last leads to the conquest of the Principality of Wales by King Edward I of England. He gives his son, Prince Edward (later to become Edward II), the title of Prince of Wales.
1284	The Statute of Rhuddlan is passed, formally uniting England and Wales
1400	Owain Glyndŵr leads the Welsh Revolt against the rule of Henry IV of England. The uprising is eventually put down.
1404	Owain Glyndŵr holds the first Welsh Parliament in the town of Machynlleth
1536 and 1542	Henry VIII of England passes the Laws in Wales Acts, fully incorporating Wales into the Kingdom of England
1707	Wales, England, and Scotland combine to become Great Britain
1797	Welsh women disguised as soldiers defeat an invading French fleet
1800	Cardiff is the world's largest and busiest coal-exporting port
1801	The United Kingdom is formed
1865	The first of many Welsh farmers migrate to South America to work on sheep farms

1881	Welsh Rugby Union is established
1915	The Welsh Guards Infantry Regiment is created
1925	Plaid Cymru Welsh nationalist political party is established
1948	Aneurin Bevan announces the creation of the National Health Service ensuring free medical care to all in need
1955	Cardiff becomes the capital city of Wales
1958	Prince Charles is made Prince of Wales
1966	Plaid Cymru wins its first seat in the UK Parliament
1970s	Golden era of Welsh rugby with the national team winning four consecutive Triple Crown competitions against Ireland, Scotland, and England
1980s	Most of the coal mines and steelwork factories close down, resulting in strikes and mass unemployment across Wales
1997	Welsh people vote for devolution from the rest of the United Kingdom
1999	The National Assembly for Wales meets for the first time in the Senedd
2004	CymruX, Plaid Cymru's Youth Movement, is established
2006	Welsh Assembly is able to make laws by the Government of Wales Act provided they are approved by the Parliament of the United Kingdom
2006	Queen Elizabeth II officially opens the Senedd (National Assembly building) in Cardiff
2008	The Welsh national rugby team wins the Grand Slam, beating England, Scotland, Ireland, Italy, and France in the Six Nations competition
2010	The Ryder Cup golf competition between America and Europe takes place at Celtic Manor golf course. Europe Wins!

Glossary

breed bear offspring; a word usually used for animals or birds

cockle small sea creature with a shell, that can be eaten.

colony country ruled from afar by another country

conquest complete takeover and rule of another country

constituency area represented by a Member of Parliament

culture practices, traditions, and beliefs of a society

currency banknotes and coins accepted in exchange for goods and services

devolution transfer of power from a central government to a regional one

disused no longer used

drover person who drives cattle or sheep to market

economy to do with money and the industry and jobs in a country

eisteddfod Welsh arts festival

elect choose by voting. People elect a person to represent them in Parliament.

endangered in danger of extinction

estuary where a river meets the sea

export sell goods to another country

generate create, make, produce

Great Britain England, Scotland, and Wales

habitat environment where a plant or animal is found

hold office have an official government job

hydroelectric electricity created by water pressure

import buy goods from another country

incentive encouragement or reward, often financial

industrialized well developed production methods

Industrial Revolution changes that took place in how goods were made, from small scale production by people to large factories in which machines did most of the work. The Industrial Revolution began in the late 1700s in England.

insurance protection

marine of the sea

medieval describing something that happened or came from the 5th to 15th centuries

minstrel historic musical entertainer

multicultural mix of people from different cultures and countries

multinational from many different countries

national exam exam taken by all pupils of the same age across the country

Nationalist person or group wanting a strong national identity and government

noble belonging to a high and powerful social class

of yore long ago

parliament ruling body of a country where laws are made

pensioner person who has retired from work, usually aged over 65

policy idea and course of action

prescription written order for medicine

renewable can be used again, not likely to run out

resource means available for a country to develop, such as minerals and energy sources

rugby ball sport involving two teams. Players can kick or pick the ball up and score points by kicking goals or putting the ball over the line.

rural in the countryside

scholarship sum of money given to someone to help them study

social inequality large difference between rich and poor people

submerged underwater

sustainable environmentally friendly

terraced houses row of houses joined together

terrain landscape, ground

thatch roof covering made of reeds and rushes

turbulent disruptive, troubled

turf top layer of soil with grass

unemployment without a job

ventilating system air tunnel

vocational course course which prepares you for a job, such as a plumbing, carpentry, or hairdressing course.

vote choose. People vote for someone to win an election.

World Heritage Site special site of global importance

Find out more

Books

A Child's Christmas in Wales, Dylan Thomas (Puffin, 2009)
Horrible Histories: Wales, Terry Deary and Martin Brown (Scholastic, 2008)
Stories from Wales: Oxford Children's Myths and Legends, Gwyn Jones
    (Oxford University Press, 2009)
The Usborne Book of Castles, Lesley Simms (Usborne Publishing, 2006)
Welsh for Beginners, Angela Wilkes and John Shackell (Usborne
    Publishing, 2001)

Websites

www.bbc.co.uk/wales/history/sites/kids
Welsh stories, crafts, and history activities can be found on this website.

www.cadw.wales.gov.uk
Find information on visiting some of Wales' most spectacular castles and
houses at the Cadw website.

www.eisteddfod.org.uk
Go to this website for information on the National Eisteddfod of Wales.

www.visitwales.co.uk
Visit the website of the Welsh national tourist office to find out about sights
to see and things to do.

**www.visitwales.co.uk/about-wales-guide-to-wales-culture-people-and-
language/welsh-history/st-davids-day/kids-activities**
This web page has helpful, step-by-step instructions for making a daffodil
and a Welsh dragon.

www.wales.gov.uk
Find out more about the Welsh government on their official website.

Places to visit

If you ever get the chance to explore Wales, here are some of the places you could visit:

Brecon Beacons National Park

www.breconbeacons.org
This national park is in a landscape where people have lived and worked for thousands of years and is very popular with walkers.

Electric Mountain Visitor Centre

www.fhc.co.uk/electric_mountain.htm
Take a tour around Dinorwig hydroelectric power station.

Gower Heritage Centre

www.gowerheritagecentre.co.uk
Visit a 12th century water-powered corn mill.

Great Orme Mines

www.greatormemines.info
Walk deep into the hillside and see Bronze Age mines and an enormous underground chamber.

Snowdon Mountain Railway

www.snowdonrailway.co.uk
Getting to the top has never been so easy! Since 1896, a train service has been ferrying visitors up to the summit of the largest mountain in England and Wales.

Techniquest

www.tquest.org.uk
Techniquest Science Discovery Centre is a family activity centre in Cardiff with a planetarium and a science theatre.

The Welsh Chocolate Farm

www.welshchocolatefarm.com
The farm has chocolate workshops where tasting is allowed!

Topic tools

You can use these topic tools for your school projects. Trace the map onto a sheet of paper, using the thick black outline to guide you.

The national flag of Wales is called *Y Ddraig Goch*, which means "the Red Dragon". Copy the flag design and then colour in your picture. Make sure you use the right colours!

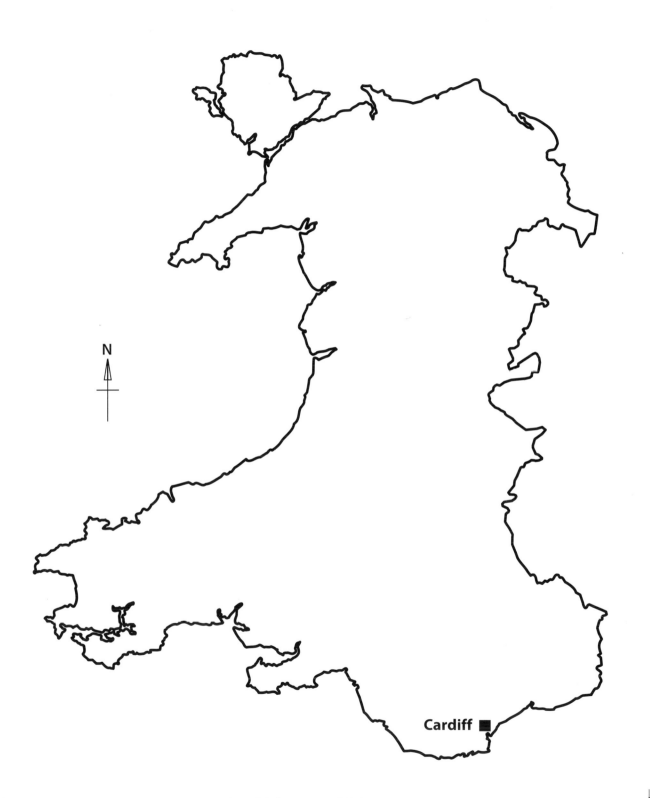

Cardiff ■

Index